To

Thank you for
being here & your
support! You're
always a treat —

love —

Sara

Mar. 8, 2009

HOWLING
On Red Dirt Roads

poems by

Sara Claytor

MAIN STREET RAG PUBLISHING COMPANY
CHARLOTTE, NORTH CAROLINA

Acknowledgements:

Carolina Woman: "A Magnolia Woman"
The Pedestal: "Red Leaf Oracle"
Miller's Pond: "Hyenas"
Poetry Motel: "One Version of Regeneration"
Sensations Magazine: "Family Secrets"
Spire: "The Bible Says, Water Holds Evil at Bay"
The Poet's Page & *Verve*: "Reality Touch"
The Crucible: "Contained"
The Moonwort Review: "Salem Pyres"
Charlotte Writers' Club Anthology:
    "Kaleidoscope: Long Road to Somewhere"
Sandcutters: "Real Desires of the Past"
Pinesong: "Grimacing Damsel Fish"
Bay Leaves: "Julia's Invisible Fences"
Reviving the Damsel Fish (Pudding House Pubs.):
    "When Roots Were Tender," "Color Their Bones,"
    "Red Dirt Roads"

Library of Congress Control Number: 2008933478

ISBN 13: 978-1-59948-148-7

Produced in the United States of America

Main Street Rag Publishing Co.
PO Box 690100
Charlotte, NC 28227
www.MainStreetRag.com

In honor and memory: Paul, Norm, Bruce;
Always—Russ and Bob

Contents

HOWLING

HYENAS

Miss Lottie Jenkins' blue-rosed black hat trembled,
her voice shrilled like a wounded hyena
telling us Sunday School Bible stories
Joseph's coat of colors
Baby Moses floating in a reed basket,
leading Israelites to the Promised Land

Miss Lottie's bumpy chin mole gleamed
like a black, sinister eye
when she told of Jezebel the evil queen
thrown off the palace balcony for wild street dogs
to strip her bones but flesh pieces remained—
her pink palms, tiny fingers—ordained by God
because once, from her heart, she stroked
the hand of a young bride

good versus evil
we learned the message well,
huddled against its flanks on the playground
as we threw rocks at the fat girls,
stroked its soft haunches
when we made fun of Henry King's lisp,
groveled with its raucous laughter
at Bobby Collins dressed in his mother's clothes
red high heels tripping in the sidewalk cracks

we felt no pity; only a throbbing in our souls
our fierce gestures, our sense of the dogs' bone teeth
raking our shins as we loped through the streets
hoping to save our palms, our fingers
dip them into holy water before Miss Lottie's
mole eye glinted Sunday next

FADING SOUTHERN BELLES

Miz Southern Belle
committed to tradition, bound by heritage
wearing a full length mink coat to a bar-be-que
rituals of mourning with sherry sedatives
wedding receptions at the country club
contradictory, confusing
marshmallow on the outside
a Mack truck on the inside
azaleas blooming in hot pink

Miz Lottie Jenkins
had a mole on her chin
with three black hair antenna
an old maid with a dried soul
she sought demon faces in stained glass
every Sunday morning she
told Bible stories to the junior girls
about Jezebel torn apart
by the wild street dogs

Miz Ginny May Bradley
wore a man's plaid shirt with
Fruit of the Loom men's boxer shorts
hair cut in a bobtail greasy with Vitalis
smoked black cheroot cigars
her daddy owned stock
in the Southern Railroad
even she knew the right fork to use
cooked chess pie from her grandma's recipe

Sara Claytor

Miz Margaret Ann Greene
sparked as a debutante
married her mother's best friend's son
with whom she had two pristine daughters
destined to be debutantes in white gloves and pearls
marry 'up' after respectable boarding schools
expected to produce more pristine children
who would perpetuate the circle
of small town snobbery

Miz Thelma Riddle Rutherford
spoke with a British accent like brittle bark
for her mother came from Virginia
she had four bathrooms in a house
with brick imported from England
her daughter always showed her panties
for the neighborhood boys
she already knew flirting
involved a ritualistic mating dance

Miz Elizabeth Catherine Stewart
married a dentist and built a Colonial home
where she kept the doors double-locked
the lights off every night at nine
no one could see her in the dark
no colored man would rob or rape her
although no such events had occurred
in the town's history
she knew race was a social factor

Miz Annette Starlings
sipped bourbon from bone china teacups
her great-grandmother's best pattern
her dyed silver hair streaked with blue
she wore high heels to King's Grocery Store
smacking gum to hide her liquor breath
knowing no one would dare suggest
she needed a hobby or a child
or even a husband who stayed home

Miz Southern Belle
knows everything dissipates eventually
branches broken, magnolia blossoms brown
azaleas blaze in short spans, wither
they know the difference
they know the truth
all bones degenerate to crumbs
not many evanescent
Southern belles left

Sara Claytor

A MAGNOLIA WOMAN

Dressed in black, I weave among fading azaleas,
a magnolia woman, smooth skin spawned in wet
New Orleans heat. When he touched me,
his hands dipped in cream.
So he once said.

Black hair laced with gray,
I glide under moss-tangled trees,
a magnolia woman. Today my gardens
reek raw, naked as the nerves under my skin
like underground roots seeking sunlight.

Once we planted a black ash tree,
dew forming clear pearls in each crevice.
Morning breaks. Cobwebs coat its dull branches.
Was I wrong to want blossoms for my breast,
petals to fall when I laughed?

Yet, this black soil fallows fertile. Trees sprout
when wanted, willed, watered. Tonight
I wear a red dress, paint my lips fuchsia,
plan a rose bed. Seek again my heated bones,
my scent of magnolias.

WHAT IS THE POINT TO THE CIRCLE?

We echo down the halls, bounce against the walls;
walk on three legs or broken knees (whichever comes first).
Go underground. Evolve into a blind fish,
the grimacing damsel fish—mute, virginal. Escape.
Breathe from your bones, jump the waves,
dive into a Dali painting. Become the tongue spoon,
the deflated tits, the snail shell brain of Picasso.
(Forget the melted clocks, persistent memory.)
Scare that wounded pelican with your power,
tickle his funny bones. We merge as one unisex:
Barbie dolls, G.I. Joe's, twisted limbs, heads, tongues.
Breed and brood.
Go ahead and show your white underbelly & pink panties.
No one cares about a fish leaping through hoops,
breathing air through fins. So, you're rare.
So is an albino tadpole,
but what is the point if you evolve upward (again)
only to hear echoes down the halls?

Sara Claytor

STRIP TO THE SOUL

Thousands of eyes have roamed my body;
they bore me as they bore into me, invading
my secret crevices. Idiots! They should be
home with wives, feeding children macaroni and cheese.

I curl my legs around the stage pole, my breasts
quivering, hump in rhythm to music. It is nothing personal.
Look at the goof leaning on the stage, light patterns flashing
on baldhead, chewing his lips like a fish puckering for air.

In the side room, slow lap dance with my sweet tush
sliding his torso, slapping hands from my flesh—raw hands,
pudgy hands, dirty fingernails— I've felt them all.
I'll whisper to his mouth, tempting with my tongue tip,

tell him lies, "Feels good, baby. You turn me on, baby."
Give him the illusion before he flips my G-string,
pastes money against my hipbone, leaves smiling.
I knew I'd take his dollars and more.

Foolish flutters in this false zone;
clatter of laughs, clink of bottles,
super sluts tweaking pink tits.
Only six more months; I pay off my debts.

At home I feed my goldfish, read Yeats,
scrub skin 'til my bones tingle, melt away
the scents of sin, seek my soul in soap,
my prayers yet to be whispered in the dark.

ONE VERSION OF REGENERATION

once she pranced naked down
Mosby Avenue on a hot August night

pine straw rustling like dry paper
beneath bare feet

her nipples like rose-bud eyes pointed
upward to the moon

a return to her childhood land
a need for the womb, to suckle the earth

later in the woods at midnight
she made love on a flat rock

stripped to birth's flesh
creamy flanks fluid like silk

exchange of Braille messages
tapping on stretched skin

whites of eyes blinking Morse Code
shoulders like quivering ghosts

with fierce fingers she almost
discovered why people have navels

Sara Claytor

FRACTURED STARS BETWEEN
THEIR TEETH

Old priests fart in their beds,
Soft rasps on rough, faded sheets;
Tiny immortal flames glinting
In their eyes.
At midnight, some pee
Against the cemetery stones,
Ignoring the dead grumbling underground.
Crescent moon like a slivered mirror
Reflecting their unturned faces,
Howling empty prayers, gesturing
Crosses from heads & shoulders
To feeble hearts.
Tomorrow they eat oatmeal,
Throw bread crumbs to crows,
Tolerate confessionals,
Never acknowledging their own penitence
Beneath the crystallized nights.

FLESH FROM BONE

Miss Lottie Jenkins
lived alone with four cats,
taught Sunday school 39 years to 8-year-olds.
Her fervent Bible tale, Jezebel, wicked queen, thrown
from her balcony for wild street dogs to rip flesh from bone.
Blue eyes glazed when she described screams and growls,
Jezebel's tiny white hand left intact.

She told stories about demon faces in stained glass windows
but liked the Old Testament best, flowing of blood,
stoning of fallen women who broke marriage vows.
Revenge a strong theme: "Eye for an eye; tooth for a tooth."
We envisioned eyeballs popping, broken teeth in beheaded torsos.

Few happenings in a small town, occasional Saturday night brawl.
Murder seldom graces the scene. Only secrets of the past
or family gossip rattle a placid surface. Miss Lottie's father
died at the kitchen table, slumped in his underwear,
face buried in a bowl of potato soup. Some said heart attack;
others said he drowned. His left hand was missing.

No solving of the mystery, only rambling town whispers.
Lizzie Borden tales of how Lottie and her Mama maybe
weren't shopping in Roanoke. Maybe the old man had a lover
who sought revenge. Or Mama. Or Lottie.
Maybe the old man played hankie-panky with his daughter.

Miss Lottie withered like a cornstalk, dried flesh pulled tight,
a mummified lampshade over bones, retreated into her aging
sanctuary, floor to ceiling windows like massive blank dominoes.
Certainly, she knew how to Clorox linoleum floors year after year,
stains still faint, muted howls hovering in silent rooms.

Sara Claytor

When she died, Richmond cousins found her daddy's clothes
still hanging in an upstairs bedroom, the pants' legs slashed.
Perhaps Miss Lottie's soul dried up, too, grass into pale straw?
We mused & mulled, finally decided Jezebel's evil a minor sin.
Who ever knows what's being weighed on the scales of the night?

WHEN YOU'RE RICH: A MINI-TALE

An only child, Ginny May Bradley's mother, a debutante
from a social & landed gentry South Carolina family, ran away
when Ginny May was 10 years old. We heard she fled to Arizona,
living on an Indian reservation, making turquoise jewelry.
Ginny May's daddy, Haywood Owen Bradley, the Third,
(now just called the Colonel & rumored to be the richest old coot
in the county) inherited monies but not manners from his family.
Generally known, he owned boo-coo stocks in the Southern
Railroad plus half a dozen business buildings in Roanoke,
two funeral parlors, & an Exxon station. Yet, he wore overalls,
usually grease or snuff stained, worn out brocade shoes,
& whatever shirt he could find, his favorite hat a once-white
Panama straw with dingy red ribbon band. That's why people
called him the Colonel.

Ginny May did what she wanted to do when she wanted to do it.
Nothing surprised the town. At age 13, she climbed to the top
of the town water tower, howling to a blank sky, threatening
to jump if her daddy didn't buy her a white horse. She rode
the horse to school, tied it to the principal's car bumper,
which disappeared when the horse broke his harness, galloped
down main street straight into the path of a Pepsi-Cola truck.
After that, Ginny May kept stealing the Colonel's rattling, green
pick-up truck, driving back roads at night, sliding into ditches,
knocking down mailboxes. Finally one midnight on the main
road to Roanoke, she zoomed about 80 miles per hour
past a highway patrolman.

The Colonel sent her to St. Catherine's in Richmond, a residency
that lasted a mere three months. Ginny May told that the head
mistress didn't like her swimming nude in the school's front yard
fountain, especially since a conference of Catholic priests
gathered on the lawn. We heard she snuck out at nights,
went to bars, danced the boogie with black men. That's where
she learned to smoke cheroot cigars, shoot pool, and cuss
up a blue streak She never did finish high school; she certainly
never became the product of a finishing school!

Ginny May sashayed downtown dressed in men's boxer
underwear & plaid flannel shirts, her hair cut in a bobtail
greased flat with Vitalis. No one ever considered this spectacle
bizarre or eccentric; people said Ginny May just took after her
daddy in ways of dressing. As years passed, she moseyed
around the countryside, now driving an aqua-blue Chevy as a
licensed driver, showing up at football games or strolling malls
in Roanoke or suddenly appearing at a Town Council meeting,
silently filling the room with her cigar smoke as board members
fingered their agendas in nervous flutters.

She met the high school's new music teacher, Hazel Doles,
when the football cheerleaders sponsored a talent show.
It was love. Reciprocated love.
Ginny May supposedly said that when she gazed into Hazel's eyes
like the color of root beer, a golden light washed over her soul.
No one knew Ginny May could be poetic, but now we all knew
one thing for sure; gossip had already burned hot for years.

They lived in the Colonel's three-story, white columned house
on the edge of town. Ginny May bought Hazel a red sports car;
Hazel quit her job and they traveled to France. Ginny May
returned with a trunk full of Paris couture dresses, her hair
feathered, wearing make-up for the first time in her life.
We heard they cooked French cuisine for the Colonel who had
started calling Hazel "Sister Doles." At Albert's Barber Shop
he said, "Sister Doles is the best thing ever happened to my
Ginny May. Now, she almost looks like a girl."

When you're rich, you can do what you want to do.
Ginny May and Hazel became an accepted couple. Hazel taught
Ginny May the right forks to use & persuaded her to smoke
filtered Parliament cigarettes. When they weren't flying
to the Bahamas for bone fishing & gambling, every Sunday
they attended the First Methodist Church where Ginny May
cooked chess pies from her grandma's recipe for the bake sales.
She even ran for the Town Council & swept the boards
with the women's vote. It's rumored, someday, she may
be the first female candidate for mayor.

Sara Claytor

CHERRY COKES & BUBBLE GUM:
A MINI-TALE

For 47 years, Dub Scott, Jr., locked in a mental childhood,
had no choice except to live with his mother Anna Elaine
nearly blind and crippled with arthritis. Daily he shuffled
downtown, bought a cherry coke at Arnold's Drug Store.
Their big house deteriorating, only beveled glass doors
under a sagging front porch rotunda spoke of past elegance.
They survived on meager Social Security income, checks cashed
by a church group that paid utility bills & bought them groceries.

Dub, Jr. would slap his mother's arms, pushing, grabbing food.
She always made him angry when the monthly check arrived;
he wanted the leftover money. Dub Jr. also relished bubble gum,
buying dozens of packs with baseball player cards, pasting them
on his dark, upstairs bedroom walls in spread fan designs.

Some days they had no food; his mother huddled in her bedroom,
mewing like a kitten's cry. Some months they had no heat except
the blackened living room fireplace fronted by two dingy chairs
with ripped green slipcovers. Yet, Dub Jr. chewed packs & packs
of bubble gum, decorating the downstairs hallway with sticky gum
as he outlined his framed baby portraits splashing in frothy foam
at Myrtle Beach, good, old days when he didn't feel an empty
stomach's burning gall or moldy sheets in a cold bedroom.

Sometimes he loaded wood at Ragland Lumber Yard:
they gave him free food; the foreman brought free fireplace wood.
Dub Jr. wanted him to be his father; he didn't remember his real
father who shot himself at a Holiday Inn in Roanoke.
Dub Jr. didn't remember much, but he knew goldfish still flitted
in the backyard fishpond, water slimy with green scum.
The day his mother died, hunger pangs gnawed fierce; he ached
from sternum to teeth. Fascinated by their glowing orange skins,
he scooped the fish in a paper cup, ate them raw.

The church group found Anna Elaine stiff, skin turning gray,
scrunched before the yawning fireplace. Social Services found
Dub, Jr. wading nude in the fishpond, screaming, grunting,
dipping stringy hair into the rank sludge. In between screeching
howls, he blew pink gum bubbles the size of cantaloupes.

Sara Claytor

SHALLOW WATER

only his head above the waves
only six feet from the shoreline
        you could tell it was shallow water
he pretended he was drowning
invisible hands grasping legs, pulling him
lower, lower into green foam

        he disappeared

roses blew away in the wind
    no Moses parted the sea
                white light galloping into me

they took me to a ward
turned out the lights
                formless fog hovering smells of saline
    earth's end
                        cannot touch it   cannot see it

remember only waving a flippant hand
turning away to pink shells
glinting in wet sand

        who will save *me* in shallow water?

HOWLING JOURNEYS
WITH ALICE & DOROTHY

Think about madness,
sorting through smoke memories
embedded lunacy like gray rocks
crumbling on a cliff
waiting for the landslide
down
down
deep
deep
dark funnels
Alice in Wonderland seeking
another Mad Hatter to make her sane.

Think about madness,
woman with rhinestone dog collar
leashed, led to her cardboard box cage
hole cut for her head
lick his ass, he gives her bread
echoes in a tunnel, she becomes
a turtle crawling down a carpeted hall
endless line enclosing no space.

Think about madness,
woman with devils inside
no answers on her answering machine
she sings herself into being
as fog   rolls   tumbles   somersaults
where trees hold their breaths
wave their penises toward a bluebottle glass sky.
The world is   paper   stains   ghosts   red dirt roads.

Sara Claytor

Think about madness,
burn every fingerprint from her flesh
drive nails into her hands   Again?
slash her like a leaf chasing wind
suck
suck
suck
mucus from her dreams
the mouth cannot pronounce; skin sheds; jawbones chew hot air
dance with Lawrence Welk, Dorothy!
red shoes click purple flames over Kansas
Jesus comes (under the sheets).

FERRIS WHEEL LOVE

Giant Ferris wheels like silver metal etchings
against the sun, blinding as they swirled;
riders squealed, music throbbed.
That's when I first met Sweet Pea Hudson.
A squall churned inside my chest;
a sulfurous match ignited across
the base of my skull.

He wasn't handsome; eyes too close-set,
small as dimes. A square line to his chin
suggested a cowboy who would shoot at stars
with his pistol. Blonde hair looked like flattened
dry straw under a dusty black baseball cap.
But his eyes glittered like brandy neon; he smelled
like buttered popcorn. When he arched one eyebrow
& grinned on one side of his mouth, I knew I'd ride
the Ferris wheel with him.

Up & down. Round & round. Blurs of moving bodies,
clouds & slate blue sky, creaking seat in rhythm
with music. One arm along the seat back, he gripped
my shoulder as I gripped the safety bar, scared, exhilarated,
feeling his hand's warmth through my sweater—warmth
that moved down my spine into my stomach, my legs.

"Look at me, girl!" I turned my head; he chuckled, both
lips wide, a flash of pink tongue. Behind his head, the sky
churning into green bubbles. I felt myself soaring
as the seat swayed, jolted to a stop at the top of the world.
Gently, our cradle rocked. Music, a dim echo as our eyes
locked in an intensity I'd never known.

Sara Claytor

"I could make you howl, girl." He licked his bottom lip.
That's what I remembered, his lip glistening in the sun
as the Ferris wheel groaned, shook; we plunged, swooped
towards the ferocity of barkers' ratter-chatter, clanging roller
coaster tracks, engulfed in greasy hamburger & onion aromas.

Yes, I howled, my hair frizzed in the rushing wind,
simmering heat exploding in my body to the end of the ride.
Sweet Pea Hudson, his hips twitching in tight jeans, dissolved
into the state fair throngs. I was 15 years old, innocent & ignorant.
Years later, other males made me howl;
but who forgets the first?

HAUNTED HOUSE

I came to this place lonely
where blue shadows flash & curl
around closet doors—
outside the sparrows praise,
screaming with joy

I am a ghost-in-waiting
my belly pregnant with sand & shells
Is this my home?
Evolving in folds of darkness,
I dream of paddling swans
on a lake of green snakes;
from the corner of my eye
another blue wisp slithers,
a smoky cat circling
dissolving into wings while
outside the sparrows praise,
screaming with joy

I swallow purple rocks
my belly a potter's wheel
grinding, smoothing into a stone baby
with your blue eyes swirling like shadows,
a curved mouth
screaming with joy

Sara Claytor

MUSING ON A ROSE TATTOO

Don't ask her why she did it—tiny rose tattoo
staining her right breast, close enough to the pink nipple
to look like a tit with 2 eyes.
Her husband hated it.

(Even when reminded of his French lover in San Francisco
with a spider tattoo on her neck.)

She could have chosen a yellow daisy on her hip
or a bleeding heart on an ankle. Probably less pain.
Yet, pain validates life.
She could dye her hair blonde, plastic surgery on her nose.
Join a weekly bridge club. Or dedicate her life to Jesus—again.
Three-fourths of her projected life span now passed.
Maybe it's post-midlife, post-menopause, ashes of inner essence
like a porous shawl, flesh sagging like a moth-spotted quilt.
Time for a twisting pathway, an untried lane, seeking
unexpected potholes and detours.

(Maybe she needs a lover who likes to kiss roses.)

But love is not enough, never enough. Old lovers linger
in cobweb cocoons, hidden in musty attics, memory bones
in rags. Photos produce no flesh heat. Today a rose tattoo;
tomorrow dried rose petals in a jar.
Why not a little blood, a little pain for life?
Eventually, maggots hum hymns in all our deaf ears.

GRIMACING DAMSEL FISH

A rare find they said, like canterberry wine, an unknown Matisse,
an older woman arching one eyebrow, knowing she has power
to choose the intensity of red or soothe with cool blue.
The grimacing damsel fish with jelly bones,
safe in herself, fearless of hooks and entangled lines,
breathing from beating fins, sinking into dark water caves
where centuries pass undisturbed until man inhabits the sea,
discovers the wondrous strange fossil encased in coral.

No man's rib bone, no man's mother, she who never
splayed an apple in her palm, who never ate the wheat
of tears, drank the blood of goats; as man chips and strips
her rock cage, illuminating her innocence, the grimacing
damsel fish stirs, white eyes roll, dormant memory pulsates:
to be alone is not to be afraid.

Fish-girl, half jelly, half bones, scaled creature
escaping from a cave, no dissections of your nervous system,
no museums for your enshrined display.
Now is your place, now is your time:
swim through caramel layers of sunlight,
pierce the weight of water,
arch your back into the stars,
engage the earth breathing,
breathing from your bones.

Sara Claytor

RED LEAF ORACLE

We walked into the forest.
You saw a red leaf twirling
beyond the sun, a sign, you said.
We lay in the fall leaves,
your wool jacket rough
under my naked thighs.
Birds listened; sun rays quivered.
The trees kept our secrets.

Later, afternoon shadows crossed
our narrow path as we
shuffled arm in arm.
We felt night's breath, knew we
were late for the supper hour,
the last bus to campus.

We raced towards the road,
our hair tangled, chased by
a black and white bird dog.
I lost a contact lens.
We missed the bus, a sign, I said.

BY THE GRACE OF JESUS

An only child, living on a quiet street.
Harold & Ella Osborne adopted Peggy.
He owned a hardware store; Ella worked in a dental office.
Harold drove Peggy to after-school music lessons,
staying home when she was sick.

Neighbors mostly saw her riding in her devoted daddy's truck.
Even on weekends, Peggy rode with her daddy on deliveries
or to Jack's Shack Drive-In, sitting side-by-side in a red booth,
Harold's arm along the seat back,
while Peggy consumed chocolate nut sundies.

Peggy didn't smile much, round green eyes shifting, especially
when she was eating. By fifth grade, Peggy weighed 160 pounds,
green eyes like bobbing apples above three chins. She never dated,
no close girlfriend. At high school graduation, she wore a size 28
dress, clothes ordered from a big woman's catalogue.

Classmates and teachers never knew much about Peggy;
she seldom spoke in classes, never attended sports' events,
only participated in the school band. She played the flute, eyes
closed as sweet, pure sounds floated into space. Peggy slipped
into another world when she placed that flute to her lips.

After she left for college, neighbors didn't see her again
until Harold died. Slimmer, she could buy rack clothes.
Ella looked like a dried weed, wrinkled face, bones sharp
under parched skin. Rumors she drank Jack Daniels straight.
In two years, she followed Harold. Eventually, Peggy went
to divinity school & the truth finally known.

Sara Claytor

First a newspaper article, then a magazine feature story. According to Peggy, since she accepted the saving grace of Jesus, she could reveal: her father sexually abused her from age three until she entered college. A pastoral counselor, Peggy works with troubled kids at a large Baptist church in Chicago. She's now a size 12.

WHAT THE CHILDREN KNOW

We can't tell what the children know.
Something lies half buried under
their vulnerable skins, something
twisting through sinew and bone,
something that marbles the heart with bruises.

Nothing's ever remembered whole;
children's dreams jumble into fragments—
yellow cars in pantry, snake swimming
in bathroom sink, purple moons
crashing down chimney.

Their memories are more frightening,
speaking through heaving seas, briar patch roads,
broken mirrors. Image of child on tricycle,
running away from home. Why?
Darkling room, pain, unknown sounds. What?

This town seems small enough but
only the children seem to know that
mothers shouldn't lie naked in the bathtub,
door unlocked, like enticing mermaids
crooning about forbidden harbors, secret caves.

In a place between places, the children
know that daddies shouldn't comment about
their daughters' little nipples or whip a
belt buckle like a hissing black snake,
drawing blood bites in tender flesh.

Sara Claytor

We can't tell what the children know
until they smother in the fumes,
shrivel in the flames of acts so heinous,
even Mother Mary wraps a shroud
around her face, turns away,
unable to bear the silent cries.

SALEM PYRES

howling in shrill staccato bursts
her eyes white holes against the flames,
she bathed in its warm arms
no longer hearing the whispers of vanquished priests
waffling through gray light

her breast milk flowed rivets of lava
tender mounds once singed by her baby's tongue
the babe who would never remember
life heat from the
cold witch's tit

her eyes lost from their sockets
purified in a sheet of fire
she heard Ezekiel's heavy hammer
echoing on the stone air
she yearned for consummation

she found joy in burning
as did the righteous
whose work was never done
who twittered at her freckled arms'
red flesh illuminating their uplifted eyes

better to be guilty, to be burned utterly
to enter heaven complete
leaving no shred of white bone scorched
no heart smoldering black
ashes to ashes sifted by the wind

Sara Claytor

yet something would be left
a toe, a finger
the tip of an ear
extremities from the extreme;
everything is imperfect
nothing burns evenly

THE LAST TABOO

Buried deep in the human mind,
an urge quivers to eat each other.
Lovers nibble lovers' flesh; babies
so cute we could eat with a spoon;
we eat our hearts out with envy.

Sometimes serial killers relish parts
of their victims, a nipple swallowed,
fingers boiled in a stew. In isolated
Wanzee the Chinese ate their
teachers who were enemies of Mao.

Rituals of old in some cultures:
feed on an enemy's brains
absorb his knowledge;
feast on a relative's heart
consume his soul.

Facing starvation, we ingest corpse flesh
weep, wail, accept the ultimate
revulsion for its moment; then
somewhere between clouds and shadows
turn again to our daily affairs.

Sara Claytor

SECOND-HAND REDEMPTION

decadent
sensible
well-worn
secret sole sins

who wore these thrift shop shoes?
   an aunt on her wedding day
   a flamenco dancer tapping with silver heels
   some old man shuffling
                      in a potato field
      armpits circled with sweat

perhaps a whore tottering
              on five inch stilettos
    rabbit coat
    fishnet stockings
    purse bulging with condoms

the cowboy boots
    of a child
howling, pretend dying behind the
                 mulberry bush
Indians at the O.K. WOODPILE

teenager in knee-high black plastic boots
mini skirt
hair in frizz
           shaking her booty to rock n' roll
    smoking a toke in a pick up truck

repair
the broken heels
nail the sides tight
shine the toes
mend the soles whole

blue suede shoes
boots made for walkin'
golden skippers
for
dancing in the dark

all God's chil'en got soles

Sara Claytor

ON RED DIRT

AFTERNOON THOUGHTS
LISTENING TO IRISH PIANO

Sometimes her face wrinkles looked
like folds of soft leather;
her breasts sagged like water-filled balloons

inside her flowered dresses
while she rolled biscuits,
flour spattering her cheeks,

covering hands to wrists
like white lace gloves. Outside
the screened kitchen door,

cat families brushed against
each other, pressed pink noses
into the wire mesh, smelling

butter beans boiling on the wood
stove, ham spitting in the oven.
I wish I could remember impulsive

moments when she laughed at the kittens' antics
or entwined purple lilacs in my long blonde hair,
blossoms as big as fists from the garden gate bush;

perhaps read us fairy tales, showed us the baby
rabbit nest, or even told stories
of her childhood and her mother's full name.

An emotional enigma, too aloof to be personal,
this big woman set the tone for generations,
played discordant notes without music.

Known for hoarding every nickel, as well
as her feelings, her tight thrift became our
inheritance, our one defined lingering legacy.

For never did she shed a tear seen by any shrieking
grandchild, or hug us warmly, or even let-down
her hair—except to wash it in the backyard tin pail.

Sara Claytor

GENES TRANSPLANT # 1

A cold woman, our Scotch-Irish grandmother,
judgmental, negative, never pleased— the family
jewels passed for generations, every relative
inherited a glittering bauble.
As children, we feared the truth,
bloated with boiling bile, invisible scars festering,
absorbed our kin's tongue abuse,
wondered as adults, who went how much further?
Was that a black eye on a cousin's daughter?
Why does one cousin never come home?
Can we count the slit wrist scars? the bottles of pills?
A black blight cowered somewhere in the past;
anger like hungry, cawing crows pressing, depressing;
we heard them rip each other's flesh,
then profess blood thicker than their rancor.
What viper poisoned their flesh? What cankerworm
bored into their bones?
Hide, hide, hide. Smile, smile, smile.
Spotless reputations worn like white vests, too easy to soil.

MEMORY BONES

My rivers flow to the moon;
my memories a weight of granite.
If my soul were made of bones, I would hear it crack.

You always touted the negatives of me.
I was blue; born dead.
Country doctor brought me back from death to future death.

Why do I remember no smiles, no laughing,
no warmth, only mirrors of disapproving grimaces?
I became a child stitched together with twine.

A black woman became my mother. Told me haint stories,
twisted off chickens' necks, flopping blood in the backyard.
You seemed a jellyfish with stinging tentacles.

Did you never please your mother with the frowning face,
your soul insulated with fiberglass?
Were you born on a day God slept late?

What use is memory or a river without a name,
when there is no end to either?
Ask how heavy is a soul.

Sara Claytor

CLOROX & CLEAN APRONS

A white lady, Miz Lucy King, a widow in poor health
who shuffled with one hip higher than the other,
raised Julia, orphaned at age six.
Almost white herself,
Julia's skin looked like coffee laced with half cream,
her eyes gleaming like burnished teak.
She stayed in a small bedroom built off the side porch.
Besides being an excellent housekeeper,
Julia learned to cook, garden, can tomatoes,
iron and sew to perfection.

She walked to the colored school across the railroad tracks
from Miz King's house. After the 6th grade, she worked
as a domestic in various homes around our little town.
At age 14, she married Joe Tant; "A 'good' colored man,
works hard and knows his place," according to Joshua Hurley,
righteous white minister of the First Baptist Church.

Daily, Julia wore red rickrack trimmed aprons in hues of aqua,
yellow & green, cast-off cloth scraps from white matrons.
Known for her cleanliness, she always smelled like Clorox
& the sunshine of line-dried clothes. My white mother wanted
a "clean-smelling nigger" in her house, one without Vaseline
coated hair. Julia met the criteria, became our all-round
household help, my nanny, my black mother, eventually
my real mother.

JULIA'S INVISIBLE FENCES

When I smell Clorox, I see your teeth simmering
like bone ash on asphalt, your head cap of pigtails
tinted red, the freckles scattered across your cheeks.

You were my black mother in starched fruit-patterned
aprons, pink velveteen palms flashing as you fluted
piecrusts, ironed white sheets with perfect edges.

You told me haint stories, sewed colorful feed sack
dresses for my dolls, introduced me to radio hymns,
gospel, boogie beats. Together, we sang for Jesus,
clapping our hands, shaking our shoulders.

Once I went to your African-Methodist Church
where we danced in the aisles and shouted Amen's.
I ate three pieces of chocolate cake at the noon lunch.
Stomach aching, I was sick in the outhouse while you held
my head. Afterwards, the church ladies fed me ice cubes
and gushed over my long, blonde curls.

On the screened back porch, the white mother served you
food in a stained tin plate, iced tea in a Mason jar. Your
bathroom was behind the garage. The white mother always
checked to see if you had stolen her dime store jewelry.

You didn't know pain in your belly from me or a stretching
of the thighs; no one told me about invisible fences
separating mother loves.

Sara Claytor

Part of my heart moved down that red dirt road to your house with its blue porch rocking chair and yellow birdhouse nailed above the tin roof. I was your 'baby gal,' even after I graduated from college, visited you last in a nursing home where you kept a photo of blonde three-year-old me tacked on the wall above your bed— right beside the picture of a white Jesus.

MIXED BLOOD IS BEAUTIFUL

and I wanted to be black or more black than white
for black wore warm as Julia's lap, warm like her
hand holding mine when we walked downtown
to Arnold's Drug Store on flushed autumn mornings,
collecting colored leaves fluttering across sidewalks
like patchwork blocks in hues of orange, red, gold—
warm as the freshly ironed sheets she carefully creased
into folds, warm like her cheek freckles as I connected the dots.

Mixed blood is beautiful
and I wanted pigtails in my blonde hair twisted
into tiny curlicues, held tight by yellow & blue
barrettes shaped like hearts that Julia bought
me at Rose's dime store where on one of our
downtown trips, I stole two red hair ribbons
splattered with gold glitter, wrapped them in used
Christmas paper, gave to Julia who quickly grabbed
my arm, double-timed back downtown to Rose's.
Prodded by Julia, I handed the bows to a clerk,
my head bowed as I whispered sorry.

Mixed blood is beautiful
and I cried all the way back home, sniffled
even when Julia rocked me on the back porch,
lectured about what is right and how Jesus
loved all little children.

Sara Claytor

MOTHER

Her iron glides over wrinkled cotton shirts
creating a satin smooth sheen.
Humming & swaying
with the radio music,
she smiles at her baby gal
dressing paper dolls—
a mother, a father, a boy, a girl.
Her boy is sixteen, lone survivor
of seven male babies, all dying
before age two, their lungs gasping,
eyes rolled back, only white holes
in their dark skin, blank stares
at a quick world.
Tall, slender, her lone son excels
at the black high school as a baseball
star. She wants him to go to college.

All afternoon, she sprinkles clothes,
her iron a tool of perfection—
skirt pleats in rows as precise as her
fluted pie crusts. Only after handkerchiefs,
blouses, towels in neat piles, she brushes
damp hair strands from her forehead,
gazes for a moment across the backyard
garden at white pole bean flowers
nodding in fading sun.

WIND BLOWS WHERE IT CHOOSES

The day my father was buried, wind blew so hard
floral wreaths on his fresh grave mound lay flat
and scattered. They called him the Professor
in his early school administrator years, glowing years
before the bedroom became his kingdom of death.

He rested on clean sheets, turned 3 times a day
to prevent bed sores; tubes in his belly below
protruding rib bones as piece-by-piece his flesh
melted, cheekbones like spear handles, teeth
rotting into yellowed corn kernels.

In the last weeks, his hospital room echoed with throat gutturals,
persistent death rattles, rising and falling in volume,
punctuated by whimpers like an unknown swamp night creature.
Those final predawn hours when his esophagus finally
tightened, closed, failed, he was alone.

The wind blows debris—scraps of newspapers,
plastic cups, empty cigarette packs. Messages
from the dead float in the wind. Strengths should linger;
weaknesses interred with bones, silent dust rising
from the ground, releasing no responses.

When I said a final good-by, he didn't answer.
Sometimes when the wind blows where it chooses,
moaning and humming down my chimney,
I seem to recognize garbled words,
listen for his voice.

Sara Claytor

THE DAY OF HIS FUNERAL

two events occurred:
we buried the Professor under a blanket of yellow gladiolas,
replacing his body molecule by molecule with bits of earth;
I met Julia's adult son Eddie, freckles across his cheeks,
skin the color of root beer, who eulogized how the Professor

invited him to the white high school baseball practice;
while he slammed each pitch over center field, members
of the Lion's Club observed, persuaded to establish a stipend
to help Eddie attend the black university in Greensboro.

White men didn't do such in the late 40's;
white men didn't do such for years to come.
The Professor set a standard he didn't know.
In the heat of hurt, a prelude to an unknown vision.

As the sky roiled with black clouds & pecan trees bruised
in the wind, Eddie exalted the Professor. I knew a deeper truth.
Julia swayed the Professor; Julia shaped Eddie's life and mine.
I grew up an only child with a black brother I never knew.

Yet, I have a photo: Eddie in a blue suit,
me in my purple dress, solemn faces captured
on a stormy June day when hard rain, like angry tears,
tore holes in the yellow gladiola petals.

WE PLAYED SPIN THE BOTTLES

Julia knew the family secret even before I knew it was a secret.
She knew where the white mother hid her whiskey bottles.
Top shelf of the bathroom closet, behind a big box of Kotex.

As a teenager, I searched in odd corners— broke bottles
in the doghouse, in the basement under coal piles, cradled
inside hatboxes. The Professor always cited a cliché excuse:
"Your mother's health is delicate."

Julia knew the other family secret, too. I was 4 or 5 when
it started, right before the white mother stopped working,
before she went away to the hospital in Richmond.
She used one of the Professor's belts;
the belt buckle left purple welts and cuts on my legs & back.
She told that I fell
down the basement stairs.

For years afterwards, I hid yellow-green pinch
bruises on my upper arms. Then, for a time, I was invisible,
the white mother preoccupied with rashes
on her thighs, hair falling out, vomiting, constipation.
When she focused again,
she began to doctor me
with doses of castor oil and milk magnesia,
monitor my bowel movements,
inspect my private parts.
I told Julia
who told the Professor who told the white mother
who told me that I was an ungrateful child
who made up stories and God would curse me, and the nigger.

Sara Claytor

I learned when to anticipate her 'fits.'
The cleansing of me behind closed doors—
I was eight the day I slammed, locked the bathroom door,
screamed, "You won't do that to me again!"

The next time our flesh touched— the day we buried the Professor,
an obligatory act for funeral moaners;
even then,
my body tense and stiff.

THE BIBLE SAYS, WATER HOLDS
EVIL AT BAY

in the white bathroom
steam stifles nerve endings

a woman preparing for evil
breathes through slit eyes

wet towels, slick skin, the smell
of Vaseline suffocating

you become a deaf cobra, with no ears
never hearing the voice of charmers

think about beaches with seagulls thick in the air
fish eggs drying on hot sand

shivering on cold porcelain
a snake's molt, a time of turning

water contains evil; water preserves life
the two cancel each other

part of the soul withers, breaks off, blows away
now the silence truly begins

Sara Claytor

A WILD CARD IN THE LONG,
LONG PICTURE SHOW

The miasma of a tangled house.
I lived inside a Dali painting: tongues popping out of eggs,
eyeballs hanging in space, fingernails with gaping faces
& Julia explaining how babies grew

from eggs inside a mother's body, assurance I wasn't dying
when my first period erupted, only becoming a woman
who could have her own children.
My soul shuttered at the concept.

I was 14 when he was born, my brother, only three years old
when I entered college, avoided & denied the 3-story white
Victorian house, clanking radiators & plastic flower arrangements
desecrating every room.

My brother experienced a different set of parents:
in their 40's, more affluent, miring into middle-age passivity.
The white mother always preferred boy children
to control, smother, cripple.

But he learned family secrets, too. Only when we were adults,
long after the Professor's death, did we acknowledge
the nightmare incubus quivering within us,
its claw hooked into our souls.

FEEL OF PEWTER

Jail was pewter stone, cold drafts rippling chills
across my shoulders, no sleep as we clutched
each other, three white girls in one holding cell
with no beds and no toilet.

I thought the Professor would understand, but his
angry voice at seven that next morning, words slicing
through my veil of worship, exposing my years
of denial; he was the good guy in a white hat.

My mind, a movie reel flashing scenes in the petrified
Victorian house; weak, ineffectual, he never confronted
the white mother, trapped in his own denial, feet of clay
shattered into shards like snippets of rats' teeth.

Mastermind, he said. My idea to join the black students
at Woolworth's. He knew when he saw my roommate
on the TV news. I hung up, thought of Julia; white folk
churches taught Jesus is love. I knew I was right.

Disowned. Outcast. No family contact for three months.
I attended my university classes, scourged for cigarette
butts in the library lounge ashtrays. An internal jail, cold chills
rippling across my heart. A pewter moon forecast the future.

LAST SUPPER IN THE YELLOW KITCHEN

they sat
in the yellow kitchen

perfect in gravity
legs apart, eyes uplifted
breathing thin air
their shell skins eerie white
a reunion with no purpose
a meeting with no unity

they sat
in the yellow kitchen

as she burned fried cornbread
hands quivering over popping grease
warming barbecue chicken from the deli
years since the trio had been alone
since her aprons smelled
of sunshine and starch

they sat
in the yellow kitchen

while the father's ghost hovered
like a titan clutching a golden ship bow
pitchfork aimed to split the sky
fallen god to one; sick demigod to another
his words whispered in their pores
coiled through their bones like a skeletal serpent

they sat
in the yellow kitchen

spoke of collard greens
whatever happened to sybil sherman
chewing dry chicken
with bumps like a dead man's skin
ignoring the rubble of past times,
sordid details of unspeakable acts

they sat
in the yellow kitchen

nibbling store-bought biscuits
dry paste sticking between their teeth
thickening their tongues
into mumbles over coconut cream pie
no words spoken of past blood spilled,
in the grass and snow, ripped hearts

they sat
in the yellow kitchen

faces like a wedding cake
left out in the rain
waiting for the Roman centurion
to pierce their sides
waiting for a staggering flash of light
waiting for ending credits
as the screen darkens, stage curtain closes
EXIT signs blink red

Sara Claytor

TIME IS A RED HAIR BOW

Her kidneys didn't function properly, diabetes,
one foot already amputated.
With her husband Tom long dead,
his niece Claudine looked after Julia.
She didn't want to move to New Jersey
with her son Eddie's family.
Too many people & too noisy, she said.
My later college years in another state,
visits became sporadic: holidays, quick phone calls.

That last day, heavy heat and odors
of Lysol and urine fused in the nursing home halls.
Pink rimmed eyes, her hair white now as the thick
linen table cloths she washed & ironed for years,
always for others, never dining with one on her table.
Frail fingers held my hand, a smile when I dropped
a Christmas paper wrapped gift in her lap.

She knew.
I opened it, held up gaudy red hair bows
bought and paid for at JC Penney's.
I pinned one above each of her ears.
Laughter when she looked in a hand mirror.
"Law, chile! Looks lik I gots red ears!"
I left her fingering the red bows;
in the hall whispers with Claudine;
she might lose her whole leg.

Driving away, I thought about Eddie
hitting those home run baseballs,
Julia's grin reading his college acceptance letter,
a bouquet of wild daises she picked for me
when I read a 100 books in the first grade.
Sometimes, even stripped naked in the sun,
our stalks survive.

Sara Claytor

BLUE ROCKING CHAIR

She lost her leg,
wanted to return to her tin-roofed cabin
with the blue rocking chair on the porch.
Working daily in a cotton mill, Claudine
spent nights with her. I was in Zimbabwe,
a Peace Corps teacher,
when I received Claudine's letter
detailing the 2-month-old news of Julia's death.

Perhaps Julia rolled her wheelchair to the kitchen,
boiling water for coffee, loose sleeves brushed
against a heated stove coil.
By the time the fire department arrived—
the old wooden structure eaten by flames,
tin roof buckled and flattened,
blue rocking chair reduced to blistered sticks.

During the next year, I recovered,
feeling more black than white,
my skin & hair darkened by fierce African sun,
my heart involved with 15 black children
who called me 'Mama Blanche,' who learned
to speak English with a Southern accent,
celebrated my 23rd birthday singing Dixie.

In each face, I saw myself on a day
when I sat in the blue porch rocking chair
beside a tin bucket of pink petunias,
helping Julia shell butter beans,
smiling in the sun while she hummed hymns,
dropped the empty hulls
into a brown paper bag.

LIFE LINES

The Professor died with my lipstick on his forehead.
I talk to light bulbs, but he left me in the dark again.

Some bones are too close to the skin,
rattling with echoes against stone

as this madness called family rips like wet newspaper
in my mind, sticks to my body with odors of whiskey

& burnt matches, a flicking of snakes' tongues, a landmine
in memory bouncing like a pinball machine's silver orb.

All the fury and mire of their lives now reduced
to chips of vertebrae tangled in the roots of an oak tree.

We burn away thoughts, cauterize wounds, insulate
with scar tissue, broken necklaces spread across our flesh.

Sara Claytor

WHEN ROOTS WERE TENDER

Who were these people sprouting with our lives,
our narrow cosmos a Picasso canvas of cubes & lines,
disjointed flesh fragments?

What seeds were sown, buds germinating?
who tended our bone gardens, footprints
tattooed on our red dirt roads?

In growing seasons, our unopened pods
contain soft teeth, our roots tender
as fragile shards of stained glass.

Later we learn, the world murmurs with whispers,
dry days, daffodils in snow, burnt pewter moons;
summer always comes, no mater what.

We found allies who could love our fragilities,
sowed seeds, transplanted genes, hoping our children
never hear the cobra's flute or see him dance.

ROADS

REALITY TOUCH

lapses of reality simmer in California
people lounge in restaurants
talking so loud, always talking
talking about going
to Los Casos or Santa Rosa
while the rocks near San Berdo
look like clumped beige ladyfingers

my girlfriend sticks party favors
in her lamp shades, hides 11 gas credit cards
from her husband who keeps black leather clothing
hidden from her

business opportunities abound
fake nails, sweatshirts, tremendous trivia
while on the desert near Apple Valley
Trigger's stuffed form dries and flakes
old beer cans lie wounded like broken bones

my girlfriend frets about her bills
takes toilet rolls from hotel rooms
stores her suede skirts in a plastic basket
she never counts dead dogs on the freeways

but maybe, just maybe
to the north, towards the mountains
splicing the sky— trees exist
logs with skins of yellow specks
ghosts with ash-white limbs
like an albino Chinese dragon
muted, twisting, humping
on a path of pine needles
slick as wax paper

REAL DESIRES OF THE PAST

A white stone birdbath left behind
where crows never balanced;
when a crow flies, the clock strikes,
the devil has his due.
Remember curtains puffing in the breeze,
dust powdered leaves of oak trees,
gazing up at a sky marbled with yellow-maroon clouds?
Remember red dirt roads, mud on tires,
mosquitoes with pipe cleaner legs, droning?
No bones in your milk, only a weeping girl
believing vinegar reeked from Jesus' tattered body,
fearful earth understood the madness of it all.
Back then, you could read pores of rocks,
recognize leaves shaped like crosses,
smell blood wounds in wild onions.
Most of all, if you could return,
you would be there screaming
when Elvis left the building.

Sara Claytor

KEEPING COMPANY WITH GHOSTS

We ride a motorcycle in the
California desert; leaning with your
torso in road curves, my breasts pressed
against your broad shoulders, my legs bare
in platform shoes, bleached hair matted
& mangled by the wind.

We pass dented beer cans, McDonald
burger wrappers flapping with gray wings
in our wake. Jet streams like long, white
zippers shred an endless sky. You tell me
rattlesnakes lay eggs under cacti.
I almost believe you.

Wind blows red as orange sand flashes.
Scorpions shuffle with razor blade arms.
We lie on chalky sand, drink rosé wine,
cold from your lunch pail, hearing wind's
wires connecting body and soul. Somewhere
across the empty highway, a dog barks.

A car slows down, one passenger waves
a pale palm as we dance a two-step barefooted.
You say apparitions wander with the tumbleweeds.
The sky looks as white as bone.
Far across the horizon, mountains shimmer
through misty gauze.

We try to stand on our heads, make funny faces,
knowing sunset to come will deepen the silence
separating our lives, your eyes lost in moon-crater sockets,
a desert bigger than God. Someday, in our own sweet places,
we will dissolve into vaporous tumbleweeds,
disappear into a mirage.

Sara Claytor

NEW YORK IN THOSE DAYS

I was dreaming of New York in those days,
the high-ceiling apartment on Waverly Place
with Mexican restaurant smells from the basement,
our view of women's prison from the tiny alley balcony.
I dreamed about the night Susan brought a folk singer home;
we drank white wine & sang bad Bob Dylan. Sunday morning,
we were still awake; it was Easter. Leaning out the front window,
twisting our necks, we could see Washington Square Park,
that same black man in a Russian fur hat playing chess alone.
Down the street, a sign hanging over a coffee house proclaimed
Jesus Sings Tonight! Around the corner, a gay bar with no sign.
We never saw the Easter Parade, the outlandish finery & hats,
dogs dressed to match owners' array. Nor did we ever see any
movement from the dark-windowed monastery across the street.

Years later, we saw newspaper photos of the little girl murdered
in our old apartment, battered by her father who beat her mother.
In my dream she raced the streets, knocking on the monastery
door, tugging at the suit of a man walking who winked at me
but who was not a man but a woman dressed like a man. I tried
to call to her but could only muster mumbled murmurs.

When I awakened from my dream as a middle-aged woman,
I thought about the tiny bathroom where she died on the floor,
clad only in thin panties, & where once Susan styled my long hair
with a curling iron; we rode the subway to 85th Street, a party
in a nice apartment; Ginger Rogers perched on a red sofa, waving
hands dotted with brown age spots, a drunk Jackson Pollack,
slipping a grubby, paint-stained hand up my skirt. A merry time
to be 21, live in the Village & meet exciting people who gushed
over my Southern accent.

I finally went back home to grow up and drive on red dirt roads.
But when I awakened from that dream as a middle-aged woman,
I wondered if that little girl, a nameless ghost now, had time
to marvel at wet snowflakes slipping down the apartment's
floor to ceiling windows, in awe of Christmas lights flashing
on the Washington Square stone arch, hoping Santa Claus
would linger by the fireplace, sip a cup of warm eggnog;
leave her a red-ribbon gift of purple mittens

Sara Claytor

BEYOND THE RAINBOW
& YELLOW BRICK ROAD

Beyond the rainbow exist nights of mismatched stars,
valleys where wet neon rain bleeds over trees hard
as carved stone. Dorothy warbles about blue birds
singing over the rainbow, wishing on stars, waking
to a cloudless world. She slips through a dimension
hole, captures rainbow wings, & enters a fantasy
world where monkeys fly, red shoes render magic,
a yellow brick road leads to a wizard.

Generations now know the movie plot,
characters, & sing with the songs.
We yearn for Dorothy (AKA Judy Garland)
to dance with munchkins, click those red shoes
three times, sail back through a tornado to her
bedroom safety & the perpetual happy ending.

Someday, I want to skip down a yellow brick road,
survive red poppy fields, find my wizard god,
mighty & boisterous in a cloud of green smoke.
Right-minded & repentant, I'll wait for vapors
to dissolve. You'll be standing there, hand extended.
And, just like Dorothy, we'll realize—
there's no place like home.

COLOR THEIR BONES

Bones on the side of the road call to us;
we stop to read directions in red dirt:
dry bones, wet bones, cold bones, hot bones.
You say (quoting Thoreau loosely),
'Life near the bone is sweetest.'
I laugh and tell you, God rides in the backseat,
looking for new rib bones.
We pass farm ponds with floating green algae,
bones of life concealed in watery wombs.
Cemeteries dot hillsides— cities of bones,
skulls and skeletons, bone meal for the earth.

We round a bend; road ahead in fading light,
pine trees like green pyramids; across the sky rim,
solitary crow gliding. He flaps his brittle wing bones,
a shooting black star dissolving into slices of nothingness.
Is he an omen? A ghost?
Thunderheads slide across the feeble sun;
Cicadas chorus in the weeds;
Fireflies light shadows along the road.
Is it now, God fingers a rib bone, infuses courage,
ignites woman's bones with Technicolor movie magic?

Sara Claytor

SLICE OF LIFE

Tonight, moon like a piece of burnt pewter.
Your face slipping past the kitchen window, a pale balloon.
Staining my silk sheets, the maleness of your odor—
hair tonic, hint of sweat, tobacco smoke.
While you shuffle down a red dirt road, I howl at skewed stars.
Tomorrow, drag guilt around like a clanking chain.

TONGUES OF FLAME

Sun burns in my breast.
I would not flame at the stake for you;
see the sun in the water. Our days are numbered.
"Alas, poor Yorick! I knew him..."
You write God postcards.
Short messages with a pen of water.
Tweak his nose for the red road is strewn
with nails, wood, thorns and blood, blood everywhere.
Blood drips from my womb, colors my glass bones,
turns them to stone. Our cosmos is beautiful flaring
across the rim of eternity, which is nothingness;
only darkness, the cold, you alone by the water
where the sun lies dimmed against bottom stones.
Reflections blur; my blood tattooed in rock wounds.

How do I die?
Drown like Ophelia, singing
a pitiful penitence to deaf birds,
writhe in blue fire? Perhaps evaporate into a red star
or repeat the horrors of childhood,
no exit with Sartre in plumed hat & black studded belt.
Our time together is limited.
Show me your bone tongue;
speak to me in bone tongues;
scald me, brand me.
I will stumble the living roads
until I fade to ghostly dust.

GOODNIGHT, TONY

Snow slides across
our red dirt road,
sticks like wet wool
on oak tree limbs;
salt truck growls around
mountain curves.
Piano concerto echoes
as fire sputters on the parlor hearth.
For a moment, I float through the needle's eye,
a small room ten years ago,
you sitting alone at your desk,
circle of light casting shadows,
beard streaked gray, cheekbones gaunt,
a shotgun at your head;
the eye closes; your shadow dissolves
into the firewood's glowing sparks.

MISSISSIPPI FINDS A RHYTHM

Over in Biloxi, 12 black men in orange vests
in cadence with salvaged snare drums & base
drum booming. The red coats coming to the rescue;
clean up broken trees, sweep up shattered boards.
Nobody smiles, only stares at this bizarre spectacle
marching down roads of crushed glass, fallen wires,
chairs perched on stone piles, a lone sailboat, bottom up,
trembling inside a church sanctuary, six-foot alligator
hovering in a corner. Silent, surreal world.

Who are these men? Their music echoing across
desolate beaches where people wander in tears & shock.
No homes, no jobs, futures uncertain. But there's music
in the streets; a thunder rhythm bouncing against
the sky's dome. Someone will listen; shuffled feet
will dance. There will be noise; they'll make it real.

Sara Claytor

MONTANA MORNING

In the muted pink softness of morning,
I hear your whistle from the riverbank;
beyond our cabin the Montana sky &
mountains appear painted by number
in four shades of blue.
Aspen trees lean against the horizon,
moisture from last evening's storm
sheen crystal needles on their
white ghost torsos.
You whistle again.
I see the shy white tail doe &
her fawn leap through the river
grove grass, dissolving quickly
into a red-willow thicket.
You have a bite, your fishing line
a blur against rum-colored water.
He fights you, exposing a belly
like white asparagus, his fins
futile on the rocks.
I take photographs, your grin
a second sun rising
as the distant mountains
spread with amber light.

SHOW ME THE MONEY, SWEET DEATH

Wealthy (or titled) people are often named
        after horses

More prestigious names than Patsy Jean
        or Bubba

These same wealthy (or titled) people learn early in life:
        impetus is more
           important than impotency

Born with a silver bone in the mouth determines
        marital choices anyway

Wealthy (or titled) people rarely become poets
        mostly lend their names to good causes

They may drink or philander but seldom
        wind up on an empty, red dirt road

Daddy (or a trust) pays the bills, pulls the strings,
        cleans up all stains

Wealthy (or titled) people can go to heaven or hell
        those roads can't be bought

Their bones crumble, flesh dissolves, no matter
        the rich dirt or marble mausoleum

We know nobody leaves this world with a U-Haul
        hitched to the hearse

Sweet Death asks no fees, extracts no monthly payments,
        marks no distinctions

Wealthy (or titled) people taste just as sweet
        as paupers in the grave

Sara Claytor

CONTAINED

Let us muse about small spaces.
The mind. Each brain cell. Each nerve neuron.
A minute white dot enfolded in black caverns.
Yes, let us ponder small spaces—
the tiny bird's nest, a dollhouse
with miniature rooms, furniture, people.
Small fry. Small potatoes. Small-time.
Small talk. Do we become then part
of the Chinese puzzle? Box after box.
Big to small to miniscule, our bones reduced
to poster board husks. Our sex is a box:
box of condoms; box of tampons or Kotex;
toolbox, slang for a woman's vagina.
What do we buy in boxes?
From paper to pencils to shoes to detergent.
Keep a breadbox on the kitchen counter.
Save box tops. Put a witness in a box.
Put a jury in a box. Carry a severed head
in a hatbox. Place your heart in a box. Crawl
into an Albers' painting, colored square box
after square box. Boxes define life's parameters.
Box of cigars at birth; box of candy for love;
box of memorabilia for old age; box of ashes
for death— chose a casket or an urn.
These small places pay us homage,
contain our soul for the endless night,
the big sleep where we hope to realize
(at last) our soft dreams, our love reunions,
peace, not on earth but in heaven with waterfalls,
endless fields of red poppies, the yellow brick road
leading to the throne, our Big Daddy Oz with voice
booming. We find the Father, the Son, and all
the holy ghosts of our past encased in Pandora's

box. We crowd into small-minded boxes,
elbows banging walls, fingernails scraping,
breaking on the edges. We are lonely in boxes,
our cells, our punishments, our purgatory.
No matter what red dirt road we travel:
we are boxed in or boxed out.

Sara Claytor

PEACH PITS ON THE GROUND

Something's wrong with the children
They're having children
a throw-away commodity
bathroom birth at a prom
only
to dance away the night
leaving a baby boy
wrapped in swaddling plastic
laid in a trash can
waiting for the cleaning lady
to bear gifts

Something's wrong with the children
They're having children
passing through their bodies
like a peach pit
to spit on the ground
no trees to grow
no fruit of knowledge
not even the lesson of Eve
with her sweet apple
the taste of the serpent
satisfied

Something's wrong with the children
They're having children
yielding their care to Yogi Bear
& cartoon friends blinking on TV screens
ignoring the sins of the fathers
the tears of Mary Magdalene
seeking something to love
only to destroy what
cannot be regained

FAMILY SECRETS

on a knoll in the Dismal Swamp
where water snakes lurked in jet coils
yellow cough drop eyes in brackish canals,
my father's family spawned

swarthy skinned with black eyes
of velvet coal, shimmering black hair
they all looked alike except for
my father's eyes, two odd blue ovals

strange maladies flowed in this family
great-grandmother died in a straitjacket
great-uncle Harry jumped off a bridge
cousin Bettie buried a deformed child

yet growing up I never understood
why my father called himself
a Jew bastard
until that day I was fifteen

browsing in my grandmother's attic
nest of yellow jackets in a corner
sizzling, eyeing me
like peevish old demons

the brown trunk
smelling like moist peach fuzz
its mildewed relics
offering puzzles

Sara Claytor

gray pictures of men in tiny black caps
a shawl with strange letters
a candlestick
with eight holes of melted wax tears

no answers to my questions
no fist against the heart, no crying in empty rooms
a shoulder shrug, a palm upturned, a look out the window
at black earth yielding wild onions

family secrets whispered against lace pillows
while all around, the swamp concealed
fallen logs like corpses half-submerged
ancient ghosts whimpering in the night

my father preached in a Methodist church
rehearsing for eternity twice a week
grandmother left us for a nursing home crib
her attic memories fading like a fragile corsage

finally, like acorns dried and cracked, all the old ones died
whatever had been passed with them down red dirt roads
we buried them, eyes uplifted, under white crosses
in Canaan Land where soggy mildew matted the corn stalks

THE BIRDS

They invaded my life in my teens.
Then I didn't recognize what they were.
An undertone of murmurs, mumbles,
felt their heaviness pressing my bones,
knowing only they were big, black birds.
Crows? Vultures?
No blue birds on my shoulder,
no Walt Disney songs humming in my ear,
serious shadows flitting past corners of my eyes.

In dreams they ripped my belly,
tore flesh from my face,
exposing skull bones, my teeth falling out.
I stared in mirrors, stared at handfuls
of broken stone teeth, wondered
how I could appear in public.
Years later, claws dug into my shoulders,
weight balancing as I swayed
& howled through forests and rivers.

They appeared & disappeared,
whispers of flapping wings,
tumbling through sheets of hot beds,
trudging through heavy sands, suffocating night vapors.
They roosted in their nests,
flew away when I gave birth;
sunlight flooded streets, flowers spoke to me in the wind,
my skin shed into another person—understanding—
something died and I lived.

Sara Claytor

RED DIRT ROADS

Seems like yesterday we saw a blonde
in a gold convertible driving on a red dirt road;
her smile could make flowers bloom. I thought of her
years later when viewing fields of Spanish sunflowers,
their yellow hair shimmering in sunlight waves.

What was her name? I think Gloria,
who could slide into a drug store booth, skirts floating
mid-thigh, sip a Coke with wet lips magenta pink,
her eyes enticing nubile males.
Envied & admired, she reigned as the female to become.

We ordinary girls slumped in corners, our mouths
filled with wet sand, staring through the store's front
plate glass window at pigeons waddling on the sidewalk.
Ignorant & naïve, we didn't know the women we could be.

The last time I saw Gloria, her eyes like black portholes
on a ship to nowhere. I saw those same eyes
in a painting in a museum in a foreign city
where no red dirt roads glinted under sun rays.

As we age, we realize universal scenes: ghosts appear
& reappear in others' lives, rivers flow underground,
bitter winds, no matter where, burn scars,
bones turn to dust as we collapse into our skins.

Gloria followed me to Ireland where no one really dies.
I think I saw her on the Cliffs of Moher, yellow hair snarled,
leaning her body into the wind. In the parking lot,
her gold convertible, waiting to cruise into a red summer.

But she disappeared on those Irish lanes, howling at feeble sun,
cursing rain puddles. Knowing the woman I had become,
I drove toward sunshine shafts bursting with green & gold bits
of glass, a wind pushing clouds into marshmallow mounds.

Sara Claytor

THE EVERY LIFE

Nights are full of ruts
Hours strike just the same
Skies contain the usual stars

I hear a singer across the wild countryside
Songs caressing paths and pine trees
One fat white horse leans beside
A crooked, brown fence

Bodies fall into ruins
Clothes removed lose their warmth
Cats can sense a storm

I hear a child beating a drum
Muffled cries echo from apparitions
A woman in a purple dress, hands
At her throat, soul joined to her body

Perhaps even our deaths
Have some hope to offer,
A burst of red poppies
At the rim of the abyss

KALEIDOSCOPE: LONG ROAD
TO SOMEWHERE

You embrace the faith of a broken stone,
you who seek the answers to existence,
who howl at ghosts while driving red dirt roads,
twisting & turning in twilight wind almost wet
to the touch. In Hoboken, no one knows your soul's nave;
in Charleston, your skin the color of whey, they serve you
sweet iced tea in a Mason jar until the world rips
into wet paper & your jawbones chew muggy air;
Southern belles fade into sherry sedatives & hot pink azaleas.
The old lady in red high heels at the Savannah train station
knows all wounds wear warm, at the end of the road,
silent ashes on a seashore. In New Orleans, you think of Julia,
sweat marking her cheeks like dew on asphalt. On the car radio,
gospel blues. You sing for Jesus, wonder if your fingers
could still connect freckle dots on her face. You dance away
mournful monotony, eat gray mushrooms cooked in spice & wine,
move toward Mississippi where you murder a dog on the freeway.
Texas is tedium.

Sara Claytor

Drive by the seat of your pants, crouched against leather seats,
steering with your fists or your knees, Whitman's open road,
singing of yourself. Speeding the California desert, wind
& sand imitate your howls. You view tumbleweeds
like vaporous ghosts, orange clouds somersaulting on the finger
of sunset. San Francisco where dreams rise like mist in a bottle,
cable cars hold lovers. You plunge into the repeated nightmare,
city streets, dead end alleys, can't find your destination.
You wonder if in the mountains wild white roses curl on hillsides,
yellow daises sway in ditches. Hug the curves as you careen,
fling yourself into the valleys. Is that a yellow brick road ahead?
Did God appear in a green cloud or speak through the rain?
Before you head towards Boise, search the skies for flashing light.
Are you blind? Slow down. You will hear the voice.
Ghosts cannot hurt you.
S l o w down. S L O W   D O W N.